The Tarot Prayer
Companion Book

The Tarot Prayer Companion Book
is a work of my own creation.

The information in this book was correct at the time of publication,
and the Author does not assume any liability for loss or damage
caused by errors or omissions, again, this is my perspective, opinion,
and experience, so it has been written as such.

ISBN - 978-1-961185-37-1

Cover, Book Design, and Layout by Ingrid H. Turner and Canva.com
Image for wands suit: Vismay Krishna via Unsplash
Image for the cups suit: W.S. Coda vis Undplash
Image for the swords suit: Birmingham Museums Trust via Unsplash
Image for the pentacles suit: Shaojie via Unsplash
Image for Major Arcana: Ricardo Frantz via Unsplash

www.inomniaparatuspublishing.com

For Mom, Megs, and Monika

You all convinced me I'm a real writer.

Table of Contents

Table of Contents

Table of Contents

The Wands of the Tarot

The Ace of Wands

God,
thank you for the richness
of my life.

Thank you for its
ever springing forth

of the new and the novel.

Let me be exuberant
with each new experience

and not afraid.

Quell my fear
of the unknown.

Thank you,
Divine Spirit,

for the gusto
of this life experience.

Ace of Wands
in contemplation

The Two of Wands

Divine spirit,

hold me outside of comfort
that I may expand into my

highest expression,
my greatest fulfillment,

and your Divine purpose.

Thank you for

softening my fear, and
expanding my courage,

as I step boldly
into partnership with you

and fulfill my role
in God's great work.

Two of Wands
in contemplation

The Three of Wands

Divine spirit,

grant me patience
as I navigate the process
of becoming.

Help me allow space
for my creations to breathe,
trusting the pause

as roots deepen
and flowers bloom.

Three of Wands
in contemplation

_____
_____
_____
_____
_____
_____
_____
_____
_____
_____
_____
_____
_____
_____
_____
_____
_____
_____
_____
_____
_____
_____
_____
_____
_____
_____
_____
_____
_____

The Four of Wands

God, thank you for the bounty of
my life!

Help me stay in such gratitude
for the abundance of my being,
for the flow of energy

into my life.

Thank you for guiding me -
in laying a powerful foundation

for me to soar.

Four of Wands
in contemplation

_____

_____

_____

_____

_____

_____

_____

_____

_____

_____

_____

_____

_____

_____

_____

_____

_____

_____

_____

_____

_____

_____

_____

_____

_____

_____

_____

_____

_____

The Five of Wands

God,

give me clarity
during times of struggle,

presence
during times of play, and

gratitude
for my busy days

which bring such expansion
to my life.

II

Five of Wands
in contemplation

The Six of Wands

Divine spirit,

through partnership with you
I am victorious!

Thank you for the evidence I receive daily
on a life well lived –

for celebrations,
kind words from friends,
the satisfaction of success

for all of my life.

Six of Wands
in contemplation

The Seven of Wands

God,

give me strength to stand in my
convictions.

Help me to remember

always -
deep in my body,

that I am supported
and protected

by the almighty.

Seven of Wands
in contemplation

_____

_____

_____

_____

_____

_____

_____

_____

_____

_____

_____

_____

_____

_____

_____

_____

_____

_____

_____

_____

_____

_____

_____

_____

_____

_____

_____

_____

The Eight of Wands

Holy Spirit,

as life speeds up,
slow me down

to sit in gratitude
for you,

even for a moment.

Help me root in
to the expansion of my life

with reverence for you.

Eight of Wands
in contemplation

The Nine of Wands

God,

give me strength on long days
where sadness
and disappointments

are forefront in my experience.

Help me be present
with all of life,
even when it hurts,

remembering that it is all working in my favor,
and it's just a little longer now

with you by my side.

Nine of Wands
in contemplation

The Ten of Wands

God,

help me navigate the heavy responsibilities in my life –

the burdens I carry of my own,
my family,
my people,
my planet.

Help me see what is truly mine to carry,
and help me carry it well.

Help me see if I burden myself
with any responsibility that is not mine,

and give me the strength, Spirit
to release with love
those responsibilities

to their rightful owner.

Ten of Wands
in contemplation

The Page of Wands

Divine spirit,
join me in my

exuberance and
celebration for

a life renewed!

Protect me in my naivety,
guide me in my innocence,
love me in my passion.

I am ready for the world to see me.

Page of Wands
in contemplation

The Knight of Wands

Holy Spirit,

inject in me a

holy confidence

to move boldly in this world,
spreading your love,
your message,
your empowerment

to all whom I meet.

Knight of Wands
in contemplation

The Queen of Wands

Divine spirit,

work through me.

Help me channel your awesome power, which
Empowers everyone who stumbles upon me, this

vessel for the divine.

Let us all rise up!
I am gratefully

humbly

your divine spark.

Queen of Wands
in contemplation

The King of Wands

Divine spirit,

thank you for the gifts of foresight.

Help me be confident which direction to move my life.

I am in service to you through the vehicle of my passion.

I am bold in my humility
I am powerful in my charity
I am sharp in my softness.

King of Wands
in contemplation

The Cups of the Tarot

The Ace of Cups

God,
help me see that
I too

am worthy
of the love I pour
onto others.

Remind me,
through your
ever present

adoration,
that I am loved, that
I am love.

Ace of Cups
in contemplation

_____

The Two of Cups

Divine Spirit,

thank you for the gift of love
in my life.

I am grateful for

my lover, for my
friends, for
my family, and for
my children.

I know you, Divine One,
through the love of others.

Two of Cups
in contemplation

_____
_____
_____
_____
_____
_____
_____
_____
_____
_____
_____
_____
_____
_____
_____
_____
_____
_____
_____
_____
_____
_____
_____
_____
_____
_____
_____
_____
_____
_____
_____
_____
_____

The Three of Cups

Thank you,
God,

for the protection
and blessings

of my tribe.

Let me be the

support and
the love that
I require,

with an open heart
and pure intentions.

I rejoice in the union of
my people!

Three of Cups
in contemplation

_____

_____

_____

_____

_____

_____

_____

_____

_____

_____

_____

_____

_____

_____

_____

_____

_____

_____

_____

_____

_____

_____

_____

_____

_____

_____

_____

_____

_____

The Four of Cups

Holy Spirit,
help me stay in gratitude.

Help me see the blessings
even in my challenges.

Let me not close myself

to love
and gifts

because of my pain.

Instead, let it open me
to generosity.

Remind me again and again -
so I hear it clearly -

that I am love and
all of creation loves me.

Four of Cups
in contemplation

_____

_____

_____

_____

_____

_____

_____

_____

_____

_____

_____

_____

_____

_____

_____

_____

_____

_____

_____

_____

_____

_____

_____

_____

_____

_____

_____

_____

_____

_____

The Five of Cups

God!
this grief is overwhelming.

And yet, thank you
for your gentle guidance
through the storm.

Thank you
for helping me see
that not all is lost,

though at times
I feel swallowed by this sadness.

I am ready
to make my way back
to life,

and your light –

it pulls me through this darkness.

Five of Cups
in contemplation

_____

_____

_____

_____

_____

_____

_____

_____

_____

_____

_____

_____

_____

_____

_____

_____

_____

_____

_____

_____

_____

_____

_____

_____

_____

_____

_____

_____

_____

_____

_____

The Six of Cups

I am the product of my ancestors,
their lives
and their choices.

I rejoice in

their courage
and their love.

I commit
to heal their pain
and their error.

It all flows through me,
and though much of the pain I carry
is not mine,

I commit to healing.

God,
help me with this
great task for me

and my ancestors.

Six of Cups
in contemplation

_____

_____

_____

_____

_____

_____

_____

_____

_____

_____

_____

_____

_____

_____

_____

_____

_____

_____

_____

_____

_____

_____

_____

_____

_____

_____

_____

_____

_____

_____

_____

_____

_____

The Seven of Cups

In my confusion,

I trust

the gentle pull of God
to lead me to right action.

I let go

of my preconceived notions
and ego-driven desires,

and I allow the will of the divine
to flow through me,

knowing that

I am of service
through the vehicle of my passion.

Seven of Cups
in contemplation

_____

_____

_____

_____

_____

_____

_____

_____

_____

_____

_____

_____

_____

_____

_____

_____

_____

_____

_____

_____

_____

_____

_____

_____

_____

_____

_____

_____

The Eight of Cups

God,
give me strength to walk away
from what is no longer serving me.

Help me move through
the grief and
the release

of my attachments
piece by piece.

Help me walk away
with love
from anything now
that is not serving

my highest expression.

I leave in love,
and I bless the dissolution
of this union,

in faith that
this is for the highest good of all.

Eight of Cups
in contemplation

<u>The Nine of Cups</u>

God,
thank you for this bounty!

I am full of joy,
wealth,
and abundance.

My heart dances
and swells, becoming

fat and fun!

Thank you
for all the gifts
of the world,

and the gifts of your love.

Nine of Cups
in contemplation

_____

_____

_____

_____

_____

_____

_____

_____

_____

_____

_____

_____

_____

_____

_____

_____

_____

_____

_____

_____

_____

_____

_____

_____

_____

_____

_____

_____

_____

The Ten of Cups

Divine spirit,

I am eternally
grateful

for my family,
for my happily ever after.

I am in awe of the life
we have co-created

and I stay humbled
and deeply moved

every day
when I awaken

to the joys of my daily experience.

Ten of Cups
in contemplation

The Page of Cups

Thank you God,
for the gift of your word,
and how it flows from me
through the path of least resistance.

I hear you in my friends,
my family,
my children.

I hear you on the wind,
in the trees,
and along the water.

I hear you deep inside me,
and I honor the nudges,
the messages,
the love that you share.

Page of Cups
in contemplation

_____

_____

_____

_____

_____

_____

_____

_____

_____

_____

_____

_____

_____

_____

_____

_____

_____

_____

_____

_____

_____

_____

_____

_____

_____

_____

_____

_____

_____

_____

_____

The Knight of Cups

Divine spirit,
I am so grateful
for the gifts you bear me

through your children,
the humans I love.

Thank you
for every opportunity
you bring to me.

I gratefully accept
what lights my heart on fire,

and I grateful decline
that which is meant for another.

Knight of Cups
in contemplation

_____

_____

_____

_____

_____

_____

_____

_____

_____

_____

_____

_____

_____

_____

_____

_____

_____

_____

_____

_____

_____

_____

_____

_____

_____

_____

The Queen of Cups

I am a
creative and
loving being,

and I was made this way
in your image.

Thank you, God,
for guiding me

to be a true friend,
an Anam Cara,

to all who cross my path,
for however long they stay.

Queen of Cups
in contemplation

The King of Cups

Thank you for
the experiences that have made me

strong and
compassionate and
loving.

Thank you for the grace
I am able to extend
in every situation,

no matter how painful,
or how it ends.

Thank you for the steady stream
of love

that flows through me
to those I care for,

cultivated through your guidance
during the hardest times of my life.

King of Cups
in contemplation

_____

_____

_____

_____

_____

_____

_____

_____

_____

_____

_____

_____

_____

_____

_____

_____

_____

_____

_____

_____

_____

_____

_____

_____

_____

_____

_____

_____

_____

The Swords of the Tarot

The Ace of Swords

Spirit,

help me stay clear in my thinking.
I let go of any beliefs and thoughts

that are not mine.

I courageously embrace
my own view

and take actions that align
with my personal beliefs.

Ace of Swords
in contemplation

The Two of Swords

God,
grant me patience,

as I do not yet know which path to take.

Help me trust
the unfolding of my path
before me,

in this divine moment.

Help me embrace
the wisdom
of the unknown,

that I may hear
the small voice
of my own mastery.

Two of Swords
in contemplation

_____
_____
_____
_____
_____
_____
_____
_____
_____
_____
_____
_____
_____
_____
_____
_____
_____
_____
_____
_____
_____
_____
_____
_____
_____
_____
_____
_____
_____
_____
_____

The Three of Swords

God,

help me fix this thinking
that is contributing

to my broken heart.

Help me see things as they are,
not as they are broken.

I honor my pain
for the teacher it is

and I commit
to releasing the thoughts
and beliefs

that keep me stuck
in rumination, and instead

I am cleansed by this grief.

Three of Swords
in contemplation

The Four of Swords

Divine Spirit,
thank you for this respite.

I honor my mind and my body
as it guides me to rest and
recuperation.

I remember that I am at my best
when I honor the needs of my body
my mind
and my heart.

Spirit,
help me listen,
and let go of the fearful urges,

for my soul speaks to me
in rest.

Four of Swords
in contemplation

The Five of Swords

Spirit,
I am hurting.

But let my hurt guide me
to solutions, not blame.

Help me honor my perspective
and let others have theirs
even if I don't agree.

Help me resist the urge
to defend myself
and blame others

and instead, lay down arms
and let it breathe.

I trust in my ability
and the ability of my fellow humans

to work through the pain
and come to peace.

Five of Swords
in contemplation

_____
_____
_____
_____
_____
_____
_____
_____
_____
_____
_____
_____
_____
_____
_____
_____
_____
_____
_____
_____
_____
_____
_____
_____
_____
_____
_____
_____
_____
_____
_____
_____
_____

The Six of Swords

Thank you, God,
for pointing out to me
the errors in my thinking.

Thank you for helping me
adjust my perspective with new
information,

even if it hurts my ego.

Thank you for
directing my thoughts
in the way of love
and inclusivity,

for helping me
release selfishness
and one-sidedness.

Six of Swords
in contemplation

_____

_____

_____

_____

_____

_____

_____

_____

_____

_____

_____

_____

_____

_____

_____

_____

_____

_____

_____

_____

_____

_____

_____

_____

_____

_____

_____

_____

The Seven of Swords

God,
keep me be safe
as I feel vulnerable.

Help me hold this discomfort,
so it can guide me
to my deepest self.

Help me see myself
with compassion,

and see others
with compassion.

Help me
be honest with myself,
and honest with others.

Seven of Swords
in contemplation

The Eight of Swords

Divine Spirit,
thank you for helping me realize
how much my heartache is
manufactured from my own mind

and it's flawed perception of events.

I am committed to my breath,
that I may free myself

from the binds of
my ego
and my trauma,

and join the world again
renewed in my heart.

Eight of Swords
in contemplation

_____

_____

_____

_____

_____

_____

_____

_____

_____

_____

_____

_____

_____

_____

_____

_____

_____

_____

_____

_____

_____

_____

_____

_____

_____

_____

_____

_____

_____

_____

_____

The Nine of Swords

God,
I am scared, and yet
you remind me today
that my mind can tell scary stories

but I am still safe.

Help me stay in this moment,
and remember that

all is well
in the eternal now.

My fears are merely
shadows on the cave wall –

the fire is warm
and I am safe.

Nine of Swords
in contemplation

_____
_____
_____
_____
_____
_____
_____
_____
_____
_____
_____
_____
_____
_____
_____
_____
_____
_____
_____
_____
_____
_____
_____
_____
_____
_____

The Ten of Swords

God,
carry me through this dark night
of my soul.

I cannot go further alone.
I need your deliverance.

I surrender my will
to you,

that you will birth me
into the light of lights,

in this time of unbearable darkness.

Ten of Swords
in contemplation

_____
_____
_____
_____
_____
_____
_____
_____
_____
_____
_____
_____
_____
_____
_____
_____
_____
_____
_____
_____
_____
_____
_____
_____
_____
_____
_____
_____
_____
_____
_____
_____
_____
_____

The Page of Swords

Holy Spirit,
help me perceive truth:

let my mind be so clear,
and my heart so clean,

that I can see, accept,
and communicate

absolute truth

without any interference
from my ego.

Thank you for the gift of this clarity,
and the courage to express it.

Page of Swords
in contemplation

_____
_____
_____
_____
_____
_____
_____
_____
_____
_____
_____
_____
_____
_____
_____
_____
_____
_____
_____
_____
_____
_____
_____
_____
_____
_____
_____
_____
_____
_____

The Knight of Swords

God, I am ready.

Help me shoot straight ahead
like arrows

to my goals,
on my life path,
fulfilling my purpose.

I am ready!

Knight of Swords
in contemplation

The Queen of Swords

I see clearly now.

God, help me be
clear, and fair, and fierce

in my intentions
and my actions.

I understand my power,
and I thank you

for helping me wield it
with compassion.

Queen of Swords
in contemplation

The King of Swords

Divine Spirit,
your guiding hand keeps me
fair and dispassionate.

I have grown into a powerful leader,
and this is through your guidance.

Help me ever be
the voice of divine compassion
and piercing clarity

always in absolute truth.

King of Swords
in contemplation

The Pentacles of the Tarot

The Ace of Pentacles

I am here to be of service
through he vehicle of my passion.

Through your guidance,
I plant the seed of my good work
deeply into the earth,

and embrace every storm
until the sun rises,

and my purpose blooms.

Ace of Pentacles
in contemplation

The Two of Pentacles

Great Spirit –
sometimes, it all feels too big.

Guide me in knowing
what is mine to keep
and master,

and what I must release
for all of us to thrive,

so I can be fully present
in my unique service
to the world.

Two of Pentacles
in contemplation

_____

_____

_____

_____

_____

_____

_____

_____

_____

_____

_____

_____

_____

_____

_____

_____

_____

_____

_____

_____

_____

_____

_____

_____

_____

_____

_____

_____

_____

_____

_____

The Three of Pentacles

I am an innately a creative being,
and this is how God comes to
manifestation through me.

I know I am not alone,
and that all great works
come through collaboration.

Help me see the merits
of my co-creators
and work in harmony
to create beauty

that outlasts me, and
gives birth to the divine.

Three of Pentacles
in contemplation

The Four of Pentacles

Spirit,
help me let go of the fear
that clutches my heart.

Help me release my grip
on what is comfortable,

and open courageously
to what is meant to free me
and help me grow

into the person I am meant to be.

Four of Pentacles
in contemplation

_____

_____

_____

_____

_____

_____

_____

_____

_____

_____

_____

_____

_____

_____

_____

_____

_____

_____

_____

_____

_____

_____

_____

_____

_____

_____

_____

_____

_____

_____

_____

_____

The Five of Pentacles

Divine Spirit,
I know I am never alone.

Walk with me on this path of grace.

Help me see that material things
are not my salvation,

but that love,
and God through love

is the only abundance.

Five of Pentacles
in contemplation

_____

_____

_____

_____

_____

_____

_____

_____

_____

_____

_____

_____

_____

_____

_____

_____

_____

_____

_____

_____

_____

_____

_____

_____

_____

_____

_____

_____

_____

_____

The Six of Pentacles

God,
I kneel
in gratitude.

I am abundantly blessed
with of generosity of

my brothers
and sisters
on Earth.

I joyously return
this generosity

to those in need,
when my own cup
runs over.

Six of Pentacles
in contemplation

The Seven of Pentacles

God,
I am practicing patience.

I am embracing the
slow
evolution

of my life

trusting that,
brick by brick,

I am carving out
an existence

that is

abundant and
service-filled.

I am joyful
on my journey,

and grateful

to smell every flower
along the way.

Seven of Pentacles
in contemplation

The Eight of Pentacles

I embrace imperfection,
and yet strive for excellence.

Thank you, God,
for my unique gifts
and my creativity.

I am happy to
refine and grow

and share my work
with the world
when it is ready.

It is primed
to change the world.

Eight of Pentacles
in contemplation

The Nine of Pentacles

I am celebrated in my glory,
and I give it all back to God.

It is through spiritual alignment
that my material alignment manifests.

It is through living
in partnership with spirit

that I am grounded,
secure,
confident

in my gifts,
in myself,
in my soul.

Nine of Pentacles
in contemplation

The Ten of Pentacles

Divine Spirit,
thank you for my family,

both born and chosen.

Thank you
for guiding me
to my soul tribe,
to the people who

hold me gently

as I transform
and birth a new reality.

Thank you
for the safety
in my faith.

III

Ten of Pentacles
in contemplation

The Page of Pentacles

God,
I am ready to grow.

I am pulled in the direction of my dreams,
and though I do not know how,
I trust the pull of my heart.

Thank you
for a life of lessons
and experiences

that give me the foundation
off of which I rebuild myself.

Page of Pentacles
in contemplation

_____

_____

_____

_____

_____

_____

_____

_____

_____

_____

_____

_____

_____

_____

_____

_____

_____

_____

_____

_____

_____

_____

_____

_____

_____

_____

_____

_____

_____

_____

The Knight of Pentacles

I am content to move slowly,
knowing that I am
unstoppable,

especially with the winds of
Spirit at my back.

I am grateful
for the experience of years
and the depth of love

that has proven to me,
time and again,

that all happens in divine
timing,

and that I ride confidently
on the abundance
of a benevolent Universe,

which I create anew,
again and again.

Knight of Pentacles
in contemplation

_____

_____

_____

_____

_____

_____

_____

_____

_____

_____

_____

_____

_____

_____

_____

_____

_____

_____

_____

_____

_____

_____

_____

_____

_____

_____

_____

The Queen of Pentacles

I am complete with my youth,
and I am grateful to step into

mother,
nurturer,
guide,
wise woman.

Thank you Spirit,
for my wisdom
and my experienced -

it is all for others.

Queen of Pentacles
in contemplation

The King of Pentacles

God,
thank you for the faith I carry
deep within in.

I am faithful because
I have been unfaithful.

I am rich,
because I have been poor.

I am wise
because I have been foolish.

I am all things
because I have opposed all thing.

Today, I am grateful for my loss
for without such loss,

I would have no gain.

King of Pentacles
in contemplation

The Major Arcana

The Fool

Divine Spirit,
I am ready to soar!

I let go of all my burdens.

I die to myself,
to my past,
to my future.

I free myself
from the shackles of
attachment.

I am struck dumb,
I am deaf to criticism,
I am blinded by

the light of possibility.

Spirit, move my feet!
I trust you completely.

The Fool
in contemplation

The Magician

God, I am power!
And never let me forget it.

I have walked this path of

hardship
joy
grief
and love.

I have gathered to me
every tool I need

to create,
to leave a legacy

of divine service
through the vehicle of my
passion.

Thank you, God,
for every piece,
even when

I cried,
and screamed.

It has led me here
to mastery.

The Magician
in contemplation

The High Priestess

Great Spirit
lead me to stillness

Let me bask in the resounding silence
of your being

to come fully into alignment
with you

Help me to remember that
the God in me
is the same as

God all around me

and at any moment
through the doors of silence

I will find you

Every answer
to every question
is at my beck and call

in honoring the silence

The High Priestess
in contemplation

The Empress

Divine Spirit,
I find you
sensually
In the mundane.

Thank you for the comfort I find
in the abundance of nature,

for helping me to know that
I am deeply provided for

in this moment.

Thank you for helping me trust
each moment
as it comes,

not peering too far into the future
or the past,

but keeping present
with divine cycles.

I am grateful,
and my gratitude is
the currency of my abundance.

The Empress
in contemplation

The Emperor

God,
empower me to build the life I love.

Remind me
every day

that I am capable
and a God creator.

Guide me
through my own desires

to each brick that
builds the castle

of my spiritual service.

Show me
the strength of
my own conviction,

that I can inspire others
to the strength of their convictions.

The Emperor
in contemplation

The Hierophant

Today, God,
I trust in the path laid out before me.
I trust in divine guidance.

I trust the signs,
the synchronicities,
and prayers answered

through others.

I am open to the wisdom of my elders.
I let go of my need for control
and I know that with

time and
patience,

my own wisdom will birth itself.

I am grateful for the ease
of my spiritual journey

when I surrender
to the well-worn path before me.

I learn from long tradition
so that I can become the truest version

of me.

The Hierophant
in contemplation

The Lovers

Holy Spirit,
I choose love!

I choose you.

I am delighted in
all of my lovers, and
my soul tribe.

I rendezvous with my people
through conscious choosing

of love over fear.

I commit to radical faith
and am rewarded by

the people of my heart,

I am shining the beacon of God's love
through faith over fear.

The Lovers
in contemplation

The Chariot

It has been said that
'fortune favors the bold',

and I believe with God at my back,
faith leading me,
and courage driving me,
I am aligned with

favor,
purpose,
passion, and
through these things,

I am changing the world.

I trust my convictions –
they are the result of many years
of practicing my faith.

Thank you, God,
for driving my faith with passion.

The Chariot
in contemplation

<u>Strength</u>

I allow myself time
and space to heal.

There is a season for action,
and a season for rest.

I honor my season of rest,
knowing that it sets me up
to be fully present,
to swim in a sea of unconditional love.

I rest so that I may cultivate courage
for the surge ahead,
to make a better world.

Thank you God,
for this moment of presence.

Strength
in contemplation

_____
_____
_____
_____
_____
_____
_____
_____
_____
_____
_____
_____
_____
_____
_____
_____
_____
_____
_____
_____
_____
_____
_____
_____
_____
_____
_____
_____
_____
_____
_____

The Hermit

I have learned from so many,
and now it is time for my retreat
to learn from myself.

I depend solely on my own heart,
embodying divine spirit,
to be my guiding light.

By coming to know myself deeply,
I love the whole world more fully.

God,
guide me to eternity.
I am ready for the journey of a lifetime.

The Hermit
in contemplation

The Wheel of Fortune

God,
in the past, change has frightened me.

But today, I honor you
with my courage in the face of change,

knowing that everything is working in my favor.

Fortune crests of the wave,
and I will catch this good fortune
if I am brave.

Spirit, help me be brave.

The Wheel of Fortune
in contemplation

_____

_____

_____

_____

_____

_____

_____

_____

_____

_____

_____

_____

_____

_____

_____

_____

_____

_____

_____

_____

_____

_____

_____

_____

_____

_____

_____

_____

_____

_____

_____

_____

_____

Justice

Divine Spirit,
help me settle into
radical acceptance.

Help me have
patience
and faith

enough to let the the muddy waters settle.
I am prepared
when all is clear

to take just and right action

Justice
in contemplation

_____

_____

_____

_____

_____

_____

_____

_____

_____

_____

_____

_____

_____

_____

_____

_____

_____

_____

_____

_____

_____

_____

_____

_____

_____

_____

_____

_____

_____

_____

_____

_____

_____

The Hanged Man

Source, God, All That Is –

thank you for the reversal of my perception.

Thank you for showing me,
through contrast,
and love,
and experience,

that there are many paths
which lead home,

and home is ultimately within me.

I am ready
to sacrifice the tie downs
that keep me safe
but caged,

in order to be free
and in service to you.

The Hanged Man
in contemplation

<u>Death</u>

God,
I am in a long, slow decay.

Help me stay present
in the slow and persistent
ebbs and flows
of my healing heart.

Help me be not afraid
of this death,

that is so necessary
for my total rebirth.

I am in your hands, and
trusting you.

Death
in contemplation

<u>Temperance</u>

God,
Divine Source,
thank you for guiding me
back to balance.

Whatever the way holds,
how the tides turn,
the ebbs and flows,

I know that when I tap fully
into the divine –
into all of creation –

I am safe.
I am free.
I am love.

Temperance
in contemplation

The Devil

Spirit,
though I feel crushed
by my own shadow,

I trust divine guidance so that
I can integrate this darkness
in me

and learn to love every aspect of myself.

Though I look around and
perceive fear and pain,
I am guided by you

through this fear,
through this pain,

to the experience of God,
within all things.

Help me stay preset,
and faith filled,

and following your lead,
one step at a time,
to enlightenment
through this suffering.

The Devil
in contemplation

The Tower

Holy Spirit,
you brought me to
this holy destruction,

now guide me through the rubble.

Help me find peace in the mess.

Help me find life that grows
through the decay.

Divine Spirit,
I turn my fear over to you.

Hep me stay present
in the massive changes
that are occurring in my life.

I am free when
I am one with the moment,

no matter what is happening all around me.

The Tower
in contemplation

The Star

Divine Spirit,

thank you for every trial,
every love,
every heartbreak,
every accomplishment,
every relationship.

All of this I needed
to reach the pinnacle of my life.

I am ready and excited for the journey
to the next peak.

I walk with you,
Spirit,
in holy lock step.

The Star
in contemplation

The Moon

Although I walk in the night,
and the path is dark,
there is a glimmer –

that glimmer is you,
Divine Spirit.

Thank you for guiding me,
through the murky pools
of my fear,

to the light,
the light,
the light –

the day ahead.

I am mostly blind, but
I listen for you,

and your call guides me,
guides me,
guides me to begin anew.

The Moon
In contemplation

The Sun

God, I am awake!

I am alive and I am free!

It is through gratitude,
and choosing you,
Holy Infinity –

that I find deep happiness.

I am finally aware
of all the abundance
that has always been.

I am joyful in this
ever present moment,

fulfilled
totally

in surrender.

Thank you,
Great Spirit,

for the awakening of this day.

The Sun
in contemplation

Judgment

God –
it is through my unwavering faith in you
that truth is fully illuminated.

I see clearly now, God,
and I am grateful.

Even the truth that hurts,
and is hard,

it is all working for me,
and I see that now.

Divine Spirit,
thank you for moving me
out of fear,
out of ignorance, and

into truth and
into love.

I am in full acceptance,
and so I am free to choose my way.

.

Judgment
in contemplation

The World

Thank you God,
for the fullness of my life.

I am clear on my journey,
my lessons,
and my values.

I release the old me,
my outdated belief sets,
and the grief that has done its job.

I embrace this new beginning,
although I do not know where this path leads.

Through my faith in you,
Spirit,
I am free.

Through my surrender to you,
Creator,
I am free.

I trust,
I believe,
I am ready.

The World
In contemplation

More Books by Ingrid

Available wherever books are sold.

Locked in Love

A book of inspiring messages and profound tidbits for the spiritually minded.

Bitch: A Reclamation

Empowering poetry for women, and those who love them.

Love You Madly

Titillating, steamy, sometimes downright raunchy love poetry from the real world.

www.ingramcontent.com/pod-product-compliance
Lightning Source LLC
Chambersburg PA
CBHW041627140626
46547CB00031B/1111